THE PREDICTIONS LIBRARY

RUNES

David V. Barrett

DORLING KINDERSLEY
London · New York · Stuttgart

A DORLING KINDERSLEY BOOK

Senior Editor • Sharon Lucas
Art Editor • Anna Benjamin
Managing Editor • Krystyna Mayer
Managing Art Editor • Derek Coombes
DTP Designer • Cressida Joyce
Picture Researcher • Becky Halls
Production Controller • Sarah Fuller
US Editor • Connie Mersel

First American Edition, 1995
2 4 6 8 10 9 7 5 3 1

Published in the United States by Dorling Kindersley Publishing, Inc.,
95 Madison Avenue, New York, New York 10016

Distributed by Houghton Mifflin Company, Boston.

Library of Congress Cataloging-in-Publication Data

Barrett, David V.
   Runes / by David V. Barrett. -- 1st American ed.
     p.   cm. -- (The predictions library)
    ISBN 0-7894-0310-2
    1. Fortune-telling by runes.   2. Runes--Miscellanea I. Title.
II. Series: Barrett, David V.   Predictions library.
BF1891.R85B37   1995
133 . 3'3--dc20
                       95-11679
                        CIP

Reproduced by Bright Arts, Hong Kong
Printed and bound in Hong Kong by Imago

CONTENTS

INTRODUCING
RUNES

AT THEIR SIMPLEST, RUNES ARE THE ALPHABET USED
BY THE NORSE, GERMANIC, AND ANGLO-SAXON PEOPLES
FROM AROUND 1,500 YEARS AGO. HOWEVER, THEY ARE
ALSO A POWERFUL DIVINATORY AND MAGICAL SYSTEM.

Runes are equivalent to
the Roman, Greek,
Cyrillic, or Hebrew
alphabets. However, they are
much more than an alphabet.
"Rune" means "secret,"
"mystery," or "hidden," and
is related to the German
raunen, meaning "to
whisper," and the Irish *rùn*,

SCANDINAVIAN RUNES
*This runic inscription is from a
Scandinavian rune stone. Runes
are made from straight lines
because they are easier to carve.*

meaning "a secret." Runes
probably developed as
pictograms and were
normally carved into stone or

wood. Originally they consisted only of straight lines, but over the centuries, the runic alphabet became more cursive. This book deals only with the earliest and most common runic alphabet, known as the Elder Futhark.

The secrecy and power associated with runes stem partly from the fact that in most of the Dark Age societies, reading and writing were known only to educated people. However, because of their likely pictographic origins, each rune also represents an object, such as an ox, as well as being a symbol for deeper, more esoteric meanings. A wild ox, for example, represents strength, and cattle represent wealth. Each rune is also associated with one of the Norse gods. It is these deeper meanings that make runes such an important divinatory and magical system.

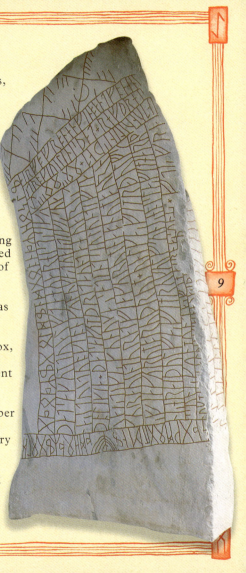

RUNE STONE OF ROK
This ninth-century rune stone of Rok is inscribed with both straight and cursive lines.

NORSE
MYTHOLOGY

THE RUNES CANNOT BE SEPARATED FROM THE
MYTHOLOGY OF THE PEOPLE WHO CREATED THEM. THE
NORSE AND GERMANIC PEOPLES HAD A RICH AND
COMPLEX MYTHOLOGY OF GODS AND HEROES.

Norse mythology includes creation and end-of-
the-world myths. It has interrelated families
of quarrelsome gods, who swap various
responsibilities as the mythology evolves.

The best-known Norse gods and goddesses
are Odin, Thor, Tyr, Frey, Freya, Frigga,
Balder, and Loki. Odin, also known as
Woden or the Allfather, is often
depicted wearing a wide-brimmed
hat sloping over his blind eye. He
is usually accompanied by two
ravens, his messengers.
Foremost among the gods,
Odin was known for his
wisdom, but also for his
unpredictability; in common
with many gods, he had a
trickster side to his
personality. Odin's son Thor
was the god of weather,

FERTILE FREY
*This statue of Frey, the god of
fertility and summer, is from
Södermanland in Sweden.*

SILVER STRENGTH

The hammer was the sign of Thor, the god of weather, and Vikings wore silver hammers for strength.

particularly thunder. He is often shown wielding a hammer, which he used to slay giants.

Tyr or Tîw was the original god of war, and some of his attributes were later taken on by Odin. Frey was a fertility god, and the god of summer. Freya, the goddess of sexuality and beauty, was Frey's sister, and at one point, his wife. Frigga, goddess of fertility, is often confused with Freya, especially in the Germanic versions of the Norse myths. Frigga bore Odin a son, Balder, who was considered to be the most beautiful of all the gods. He was an expert in herbal medicine and the runes; he even had the runes carved on his tongue. Balder was eventually slain through the treachery of Loki, the god of lies, deceit, and trickery.

JELLING CUP
Scandinavia's King Gorm is thought to have drunk from this silver cup, called the Jelling Cup.

HISTORY
of THE RUNES

THE NORSE MYTHS TELL HOW ODIN HUNG UPSIDE
DOWN FROM THE GREAT WORLD TREE, YGGDRASIL, FOR
NINE DAYS AND NIGHTS, IMPALED ON HIS OWN SPEAR,
IN ORDER TO GAIN THE WISDOM OF THE RUNES.

The runes are associated with wisdom and well-being, words and deeds, and the gods and magical power. They are both practical and mystical. Because the Norse were a very realistic people, the magical and the religious were seen as a fundamental part of everyday life. If a particular combination of runes (see *Bind-runes, pages 46–47*) brought luck or protection, it made sense for a warrior to carry it with him.

~ ◎ ~

When Christianity spread into northern Europe in the Dark Ages, the power of the Norse gods waned, but not entirely. The two religions existed side by side to some extent, and there are many gravestones and crosses in

FREYA'S CHARIOT
This illustration of Freya riding in her swan-drawn chariot is after a painting by H. J. Ford, 1902.

THE HANGED MAN
Odin is often considered to be the Tarot's Hanged Man. This card is from the Tarot of Charles VI.

used for writing, and for more esoteric purposes, for many more centuries. As late as 1639 there was an edict in Iceland forbidding their use, and even in the late 19th century, pastors in remote rural parts of Scandinavia were required to be able to read and write the runes.

Many elements of the Old Norse language have survived in the modern Scandinavian languages, and in English, Dutch, and German. The Icelandic language is the closest present-day language to Old Norse. In English, the occasional use of "Ye" to mean "The" is a strong reminder of the rune Thorn (Þ), which is pronounced "Th" but looks similar to a "Y."

northern Europe with the crucified Christ on one side and scenes from Norse mythology on the other. Often the inscriptions were in runes rather than in the Roman alphabet.

Despite the efforts of the Catholic Church to stamp out their use, runes were

THE ELDER FUTHARK

THE WORD "ALPHABET" COMES FROM THE FIRST TWO
LETTERS OF THE GREEK ALPHABET, ALPHA AND BETA.
SIMILARLY, THE NORSE ALPHABET IS CALLED A
FUTHARK, AFTER THE SOUNDS OF THE FIRST SIX
CHARACTERS – F (ᚠ), U (ᚢ), TH (ᚦ), A (ᚨ), R (ᚱ), K (ᚲ).

Just as the Roman alphabet has slight differences in some modern languages, such as the Dutch ij, the German ß, and the Danish Å, the Norse alphabet, the Futhark, has developed certain variations. These variations developed over the centuries in different northern European countries. The standard Elder Futhark contains 24 characters. They are divided into three groups, called Aetts, each containing

OLDEST ALPHABET
This runic stone is inscribed with the oldest representation of the 24-rune alphabet.

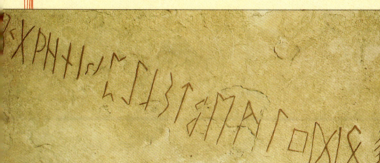

eight runes. However, there are Futharks with as few as 16 runes. The Anglo-Saxon Futhark had 28 runes, and then 33 runes, with the new runes being developed to stand for different variations of sounds.

The 16-rune Younger Futhark, sometimes called the Danish Futhark, developed between AD 600 and 850, and dropped certain sounds. This later made it necessary to create "dotted runes" to distinguish between, for example, K and G, T and D, and P and B.

Modern-day understanding of the development of the Futhark has been confused

WHALEBONE RUNES
This intricately carved whalebone casket with runic inscription dates from around AD 665.

further by the various calligraphic styles used in different countries over the centuries. Some runes changed their appearance, sound, name, and meaning.

Occasionally, books on runes add an extra rune to the standard 24. This is known as Wyrd, and it is completely blank. It means fate, destiny, and karma. Wyrd is a very recent addition to the rune-set. It is sometimes considered unnecessary because many of the runes already contain its meaning.

FREY'S AETT

THE ELDER FUTHARK IS DIVIDED INTO THREE GROUPS OF RUNES, CALLED AETTS. THE FIRST AETT IS NAMED AFTER FREY, THE GOD OF FERTILITY. FREY'S AETT CONTAINS EIGHT RUNES – FEOH (ᚠ), UR (ᚢ), THORN (ᚦ), ANSUR (ᚨ), RAD (ᚱ), KEN (ᚲ), GYFU (ᚷ), AND WYN (ᚹ).

FEOH

This rune means cattle, and in early societies, cattle were a measure of wealth. Feoh (ᚠ) means movable wealth, such as money and possessions. It also implies the energy and hard work that leads to wealth. Movable wealth can take many forms – it can be emotional and spiritual wealth as well as money. Feoh is Frey's rune, and he is the god of fertility, itself a form of richness.

UR

The rune Ur (ᚢ) means aurochs, which was a large bison that became extinct in 1627. Ur encompasses physical strength, endurance, courage, and freedom. It includes emotional and spiritual strength, male sexual potency, and good health. It can also imply a challenge leading to a major life change.

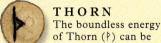

THORN

The boundless energy of Thorn (Þ) can be used for good or for chaos. It represents the forces of the human unconscious, including excessive anger and lust. The thorn is a clear phallic symbol; it can prick, stab, and tear, and be a weapon that can do great harm. However, it can also be protective, like the hedge of thorns surrounding Sleeping Beauty. It could also mean a stroke of good luck, but Thorn usually tends to be a warning that your luck is running out.

ANSUR

This rune has a meaning similar to the Greek *logos*, the spoken word of God. Ansur (ᚠ) is also known as Ansuz. It is associated with the Norse gods, particularly Odin, and represents controlled, creative, and divine power. Spiritually, it is the rune of prophecy and revelation. It also encompasses the ideas of wisdom, knowledge, reason, and communication – and therefore of instruction and good advice. Ansur might also refer to a test, an examination, or perhaps an interview. Many futharks replace Ansur with the rune Os, which can sometimes cause confusion.

RAD

The rune Rad (ᚱ) can mean wheel, ride, or travel, but it also has a deeper meaning. Riding a horse includes both movement and direction. It can be long and arduous, requiring planning, foresight, determination, and fortitude. Rad can therefore refer to the journey of life or to a spiritual quest. Rad might also mean communication, such as delivering or receiving a message, wise counsel, the wheel of life, and sexual intercourse.

18

KEN

The rune Ken (ᚲ) sheds light on the path, dispels the dark shadows of ignorance, and helps us to see with true discernment. The Scottish verb "to ken" means to see, know, and understand. Ken strongly suggests that "seeing" must then lead to some form of action, and light in darkness clearly implies esoteric spiritual illumination. Ken also represents the natural warmth and companionship of the fireside and, by implication, robust good health. Light accompanied by action implies creativity and the birth of new ideas.

G Y F U

This rune means gift. Accepting a gift places you under a certain obligation to the giver, establishing a bond or a relationship between giver and receiver. In Norse culture, a gift always called for a gift in return. Gyfu (ᚷ) can also mean a partnership or union, in business or in love. Gyfu is commonly used as the sign of a kiss – the symbol of the bond of mutual affection.

W Y N

Wyn (ᚹ) is linked to a reward – a feeling of goodness, joy and satisfaction, peaceful winning, and ultimate achievement. It contains the idea of everything going well because you are in total harmony with life. Spiritually, this rune is the ecstatic joy of closeness to God or the gods. It also implies close cooperation and companionship with other people, because joy is not usually a solitary emotion. When so much of life can tend to be negative, it is important to try to allow the joy of Wyn to permeate every part of your life.

HAGAL'S AETT

THE SECOND AETT IS NAMED AFTER HAGAL, WHICH MEANS THE WEATHER CONDITION OF HAIL. HAGAL'S AETT CONTAINS HAGAL (ᚼ), NYD (ᚾ), IS (ᛁ), GER (ᛊ), EOH (ᛁ), PEORTH (ᛈ), EOLH (ᛉ), AND SIGEL (ᛋ). THEY ARE THE RUNES OF OPPORTUNITY AND ACHIEVEMENT.

HAGAL

The rune Hagal (ᚼ) is similar to an unexpected hailstorm – an elemental disruption to your life. When Hagal is linked with other runes, it can suggest limitation, interruption, or delay, and imply a complete change in direction. Hagal can also mean suffering, hardship, illness, or injury.

NYD

The usual meaning of this rune is being in need, hardship, or adversity. Luckily, it includes the perseverance to endure, and reserves of inner strength. Nyd (ᚾ) counsels patience; however unpleasant, this is a learning experience. It can also warn against taking a risky path. In conjunction with other runes, Nyd has a delaying influence.

IS

The rune Is (|) means ice. Although ice can be beautiful, it is also dangerous – its slippery surface cannot be trusted to support you, and it can be an obstacle to your progress. Is means that you may have to delay your plans until a more favorable season. This rune can take the heat out of a confrontational situation and protect against magical attack. Emotionally, it implies a cooling of affection, or frigidity. It has a freezing, delaying, or preserving effect on other runes in a rune-cast.

GER

Although Ger (⟨) means harvest, and implies the natural fruitfulness of autumn, it also encompasses the idea of the entire cycle of seasons. Ger is movement, change, and natural development. It is usually very positive, but it is a rune of cause and effect, and may show the end result of your past actions. For this reason, Ger is also connected with the idea of justice – a just reward, which can be positive, but also negative, such as punishment for misdeeds.

EOH

The rune Eoh (ᛇ) means yew. This tree is linked with death, and it is a pre-Christian custom to plant yew trees in a graveyard. However, it should be remembered that the yew is evergreen, and death is a doorway to rebirth into a new life, whether in a Viking Valhalla, a Christian heaven, or through reincarnation. Eoh should not be feared, because it also means continuity and endurance. The best longbows were always made from yew trees. As well as being strong, long-lasting, and flexible, they contained protective magic. Eoh can also symbolize courage.

22

PEORTH

This rune can mean a dice cup or a gaming piece. It represents a game of chance and skill, symbolic of making the best of your fate. Spiritually, Peorth (ᛈ) suggests the disclosure of the hidden or secret. It could also refer to pregnancy and birth. Peorth is linked with the sensible and moderate enjoyment of sexuality. The interpretation of Peorth also calls for good sense and moderation, as in the way food and wine are enjoyed at a banquet.

EOLH

This favorable rune illustrates both the antlers of the elk, and the shape of the herb elk-sedge or elongated sedge. Eolh (†) also suggests the splayed fingers of the warding-off hand. It is a powerful rune of protection and, spiritually, it symbolizes reaching up to the divine. Eolh also has the idea of success through endeavor in a hunt, quest, or other enterprise.

SIGEL

Although Sigel (ϟ) is well known as a victory symbol, it can also be used as a force of attack. It is a positive force because it is the natural power of the sun. Spiritually, Sigel symbolizes clear vision, the victories of light over darkness, and good over evil. The common use of Sigel in Nazi insignia was a cynical perversion of the rune's true nature, which is to use the powers of good to vanquish evil.

TYR'S AETT

THE THIRD AETT IS NAMED AFTER TYR, THE GOD OF WAR. TYR'S AETT CONTAINS TYR (↑), BEORC (ᛒ), EHWAZ (ᛗ), MAN (ᛗ), LAGU (ᛚ), ING (◇), DAEG (ᛞ), AND ODEL (ᚪ). THEY ARE THE RUNES OF INTELLECTUAL ACHIEVEMENT AND SPIRITUAL ENGLIGHTEMENT.

TYR

The Norse god Tyr is directly related to the Greek god Zeus, and the Roman god Jupiter. Tyr was the god of war and justice, fair law and regulation, and success through sacrifice. He allowed a wolf to bite off his hand in order to bind the wolf's chaotic force. The rune Tyr (↑) signifies all these qualities, and includes determination and male sexuality.

BEORC

This rune refers to renewal, regeneration, purification, healing, and recovery. Beorc (ᛒ) is the rune of the family and the home, and represents the enjoyment of sexual relations, fertility, and birth. This birth can be literal or symbolic, such as the successful start of any new idea or enterprise.

EHWAZ

The speed, strength, and beauty of the horse has lead to it always being regarded as much more than a means of transportation. In a metaphorical sense, it is sacred – a vehicle for material and spiritual advancement. The rune Ehwaz (ᛖ) implies controlled change, progress, and sometimes simply a journey. It also represents partnership, trust, loyalty, and faithfulness, such as that found between horse and rider or brother and sister. They are two halves of the same whole.

MAN

The rune Man (ᛗ) means human rather than male, and the shared human nature within each individual. It contains the paradox that we are all part of the human family, yet ultimately we are all on our own, in life and in the final journey into death. Humans can be distinguished from animals by their creativity, intelligence, forward planning, and speech; this rune covers such mental faculties. It also implies cooperation between individuals for the benefit of the common good.

LAGU

The rune Lagu (↑) means water. For the seafaring Norse, water was a vital part of life and a constant danger; in the same way, the journey through life always contains a risk of shipwreck and drowning. Lagu contains elements of fluidity, mutability, and a lack of control. It represents the sensual madness of sexuality, the depths of the unconscious, intuition, and psychic abilities. Its deceptive elements come from its mutability, rather than from malignity. Traditionally, Lagu is the ultimate female rune.

ING

The main meaning of the rune Ing (◇) is completion – the certainty of a conclusion. This can include, for example, the male orgasmic force, or birth as the conclusion to pregnancy. Ing was an early fertility god equivalent to Frey. Ing is therefore associated with healthy, wholesome sexuality, a strong, affectionate family, and a safe and secure home. It also symbolizes protection and a light shining in the darkness – therefore, spiritual aspiration.

DAEG

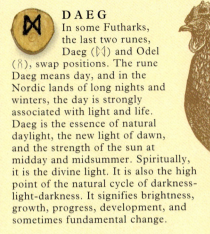

In some Futharks, the last two runes, Daeg (ᛗ) and Odel (ᛟ), swap positions. The rune Daeg means day, and in the Nordic lands of long nights and winters, the day is strongly associated with light and life. Daeg is the essence of natural daylight, the new light of dawn, and the strength of the sun at midday and midsummer. Spiritually, it is the divine light. It is also the high point of the natural cycle of darkness-light-darkness. It signifies brightness, growth, progress, development, and sometimes fundamental change.

ODEL

Odel (ᛟ) means the ancestral country or home, and fixed wealth or an inheritance. This can include your inherited characteristics – aspects of yourself that you gained from your grandparents and will pass on to your grandchildren. Odel can also represent a family's strength. It can be seen as everything that you have accomplished during your lifetime, including talents and experience. It can also represent your spiritual home. A variant form shows Odel without its "legs."

CASTING
THE RUNES

AS WITH OTHER FORMS OF DIVINATION, BY CASTING
RUNES YOU ARE SEEKING ANSWERS TO IMPORTANT
QUESTIONS ABOUT YOUR OWN LIFE, OR TO OTHER
PEOPLE'S QUESTIONS.

There are many recurrent themes in the meanings of the runes. Death, hardship, unexpected troubles and delays, struggles, and victory are mentioned many times, but so are the warmth and security of the home, and the unrestrained pleasure and deep, trusting love in a sexual relationship. The runes' originators, the Norse peoples, lived life to the full, which included embracing the negative and bad as well as the positive and good.

In some ways, the Norse philosophy of life is encompassed in the meanings of the Peorth rune ( ). After a battle, the Norse celebrated in the banqueting hall – eating, drinking, dancing, and carousing – but kept in mind that the next day they might be out fighting again, or hunting, or working hard alongside their companions. Essentially, the meaning of the Peorth rune is that life goes on regardless, and its hardships make its pleasures all the more enjoyable. In Norse thinking, fate is not predetermined; life is a game of skill as well as chance. It is always up to you to take the "game pieces" you have been given, and use them to your best advantage.

When using the runes, you should always give something in exchange, which at the very least should be your careful attention. The search for esoteric knowledge should never be undertaken lightly, and the gods or powers may demand a sacrifice from you.

Even the Norse god Odin, for example, hung from the World Tree for nine days and nights to gain the knowledge of the runes.

When casting the runes, some people draw the relevant number of runes out of their bag one at a time. Other people prefer to spread all the runes out on a table, or on a white or neutral-colored cloth, face down, and then select the runes to be used in the reading. This method has the advantage that your fingers may be drawn to certain runes. Once you have selected the right number of runes and laid them in

the pattern of the rune-cast you are using, turn them over one by one, turning them sideways, not top to bottom. Eight of the twenty-four runes are the same either way up. For the other sixteen, a reversed rune means that its most negative aspects are emphasized. Its good aspects may be conspicuous by their absence, or might be corrupted in some way, and it exerts a completely unhelpful influence on the other runes around it.

RUNES RITUAL

Lighting a candle to invoke the Norse gods and casting the runes next to natural objects might prove useful to some people.

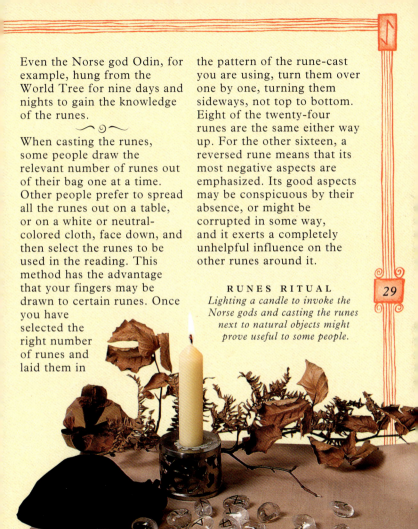

THE **THREE-RUNE** READING

THESE ARE TWO EXAMPLES OF A VERY SIMPLE READING.
AS ITS NAME SUGGESTS, THREE RUNES ARE USED –
THE FIRST RUNE REPRESENTS WHERE YOU ARE NOW,
THE SECOND RUNE SHOWS YOUR PATH, AND THE THIRD
RUNE REPRESENTS YOUR FUTURE.

This is a reading about a novel-in-progress. Rad (ᚱ) in the present position shows movement, progress, and a journey (perhaps in the mind). Ehwaz (ᛗ) also suggests travel, but contains strong elements of both partnership and change. Gyfu (ᚷ) in the future position is at its simplest a gift, but it can represent both giving and receiving. Gyfu also contains opportunity, and possibly a union.

The possible conclusions from this reading are travel and change, leading to opportunity; writing the novel in partnership with someone else, to mutual advantage; or a major change in the life of the querent (the questioner), such as marriage.

The querent's next three-rune reading is asking about the nature of the major change. Eolh (ᛉ) in the present position has elements of protection and friendship, and Hagal (ᚻ) shows a sudden, major change. There is a successful outcome in Sigel (ᛋ), symbolizing the shining sun and victory.

The conclusion of the second reading seems to be that the turbulent change will result in something positive and good. Putting the two readings together, a major change in the querent's life is likely to affect the progress of the novel greatly. The change will turn his life upside-down, but the ensuing partnership or relationship will be a gift, and the future should be bright and shining.

HERE/NOW

Rad

HERE/NOW

Eolh

PATH

Ehwaz

PATH

Hagal

THERE/FUTURE

Gyfu

THERE/FUTURE

Sigel

THE **SIX-RUNE** READING

THIS SIX-RUNE SPREAD IS SIMILAR IN FORMAT TO THE
THREE-RUNE READING, BUT USES TWO RUNES INSTEAD
OF ONE RUNE IN EACH OF THE THREE POSITIONS.
OFTEN THE INTERPLAY BETWEEN TWO OR MORE RUNES
CAN GIVE A DEEPER ANSWER THAN JUST ONE RUNE.

The querent wants to ask the runes how his life can be improved. In this rune-cast, it is particularly significant to see two runes from Hagal's Aett, and four runes from Tyr's Aett. Patterns such as these can add to the interpretation of the rune-cast.

Eoh (ᛇ) in the current position suggests that the querent is currently going through a period that seems dark and deathlike. However, he should think of the evergreen yew tree in the graveyard, and have courage to progress through rebirth. Ehwaz (ᛗ) shows that change will come to his life through putting his trust in someone else. Beorc (ᛒ) suggests that this person will be a woman, a committed

family person, while Man (ᛗ) speaks of close cooperation for the common good. These two runes, therefore, could be forecasting marriage.

Peorth (ᛈ) and Lagu (ᛚ) in the future position both suggest something hidden, esoteric, probably spiritual, and perhaps something to do with psychic abilities. Peorth implies an enjoyable time ahead, but it carries a warning of the need to be levelheaded, which is probably the best way to handle the uncertainty and changeability of Lagu.

This reading implies that the future will not be dull. There will be significant change, but working with someone else whom you trust should lead to a fascinating future.

HERE/NOW

Eoh

Ehwaz

PATH

Beorc

Man

THERE/FUTURE

Peorth

Lagu

THE **SEVEN-RUNE** READING

THE QUERENT WANTS TO KNOW HOW HE CAN FIND THE
PERSON WHO WILL PARTNER HIM INTO THE FUTURE.
HIS PROBLEM IS CLEARLY STATED IN THE RUNE-CAST.
THE "FREEZING" RUNE, IS, ACTS AS AN OBSTACLE TO
THE HOME AND FAMILY QUALITIES OF ODEL.

In this reading, both runes in the outside factors position are reversed; therefore their individual effect and influence on each other will be negative. This could be seen as a need (shown by Nyd, ↑) for advancement (shown by Ehwaz, ᛗ), but without any success or progress, because Nyd can often be a delaying factor in conjunction with other runes.

The outside world appears to be against the querent. The reversal of Ehwaz suggests uncontrolled change, and a lack of partnership and trust. The reversed Nyd says that this is a difficult time. It advises accepting the uncomfortable situation for as long as it must last rather than making hasty decisions.

The best course to get out of this situation is to go through the change, uncertainty, and deception represented by the reversed Lagu (↑). Daeg (ᛞ) is a positive, nonreversible rune, and the message seems to be that there is light at the end of the tunnel.

This positive conclusion is emphasized by the outcome rune, Ing (◇), which represents completion and certainty. It is a rune of warmth and closeness, suggesting the companionship and security of a good home.

Although this rune-cast seems rather negative initially, its overall meaning is clearly positive. The person who will bring fulfillment to the querent's life will definitely arrive.

OUTCOME

Ing

BEST COURSE

Lagu REV

Daeg

OUTSIDE
FACTORS

Ehwaz REV

Nyd REV

PROBLEM

Is

Odel

35

THE **CROSS** READING

FOR SEVERAL YEARS, THE QUERENT HAS BEEN EXPERIENCING SERIOUS PROBLEMS WITH HER LANDLORD. SHE NOW WANTS TO ASK THE RUNES HOW SHE CAN DEFEND HERSELF AGAINST HER LANDLORD, AND EVENTUALLY BE VICTORIOUS.

It is at first difficult to see how the brightness of Daeg's (ᛞ) day can be related to the querent's problems. However, by taking these continuing problems as the ongoing present situation, Daeg could refer to the time before the problems started. In comparison to the present, perhaps this time was like a bright and sunny day.

~ ☺ ~

At the present moment, the querent is seeking protection and trying to ward off her landlord; therefore Eolh's (ᛉ) appearance in this position is particularly appropriate. Eolh is a very favorable rune, implying success.

~ ☺ ~

Ehwaz (ᛗ) in the future position shows a controlled change for the better. Its element of partnership could refer to the querent working closely together with the other tenants against their common enemy.

~ ☺ ~

Gyfu (ᚷ) in the hinder position proves puzzling, because how can a gift possibly be a hindrance? Here, it seems that Gyfu has more of a meaning of obligation, perhaps of a business relationship (in this case, a lease). This is indeed the root of the problem.

~ ☺ ~

Ur (ᚢ) in the help position is a very positive indication. It represents unbounded strength and determination. The querent is facing a major challenge, but with Ur's strength and in partnership with the other tenants, she should eventually win.

HELP

Ur

PAST

Daeg

PRESENT

Eolh

FUTURE

Ehwaz

HINDER

Gyfu

THE **CELTIC CROSS** READING

THIS LAYOUT WILL BE FAMILIAR TO USERS OF TAROT –
THE CELTIC CROSS IS A COMPREHENSIVE SPREAD,
WHICH IS USEFUL FOR COMPLEX ISSUES. THE QUERENT
IS ASKING THE RUNES HOW SHE CAN BECOME MORE
SUCCESSFUL IN HER CHOSEN PROFESSION.

The runes of the present moment, Lagu (ᛚ) and Gyfu (ᚷ), affect each other. Lagu contains an element of uncertainty, but real creativity may come from this, which could be seen in Gyfu as a problematic gift.

Ansur (ᚨ) reversed and Rad (ᚱ) in the past positions show that the querent's life journey has been affected by bad advice. She could also be having communication difficulties or be moving in the wrong direction.

Is (ᛁ, future influences) may be temporarily delaying the creative rebirth promised by Eoh (ᛇ, future events). The reversal of Eolh (ᛉ, the querent's influence on the world) suggests a lack of success, and the reversed

Beorc (ᛒ, the world's influence on the querent) implies negative female influences on her, as well as outside influences causing failure in a new project. Hagal (ᚺ, hopes and fears) suggests that the querent fears the unexpected but possesses an underlying stubbornness. Nyd (ᚾ, the outcome) is not easy. It suggests that her struggle for success is going to be hard, but that she may succeed by remaining patient.

The reading recommends patience, trying to learn from past experiences whether good or bad, and perseverance. It does not say that the querent will never be successful, but it does stress that it is unlikely to happen in the near future.

OUTCOME

Nyd

**FUTURE
INFLUENCES**

Is

**HOPES
AND
FEARS**

Hagal

**PAST
EVENTS**

Rad

**PRESENT/
OBSTACLE**

Lagu/Gyfu

**FUTURE
EVENTS**

Eoh

**WORLD'S
INFLUENCE
ON QUERENT**

Beorc REV

**PAST
INFLUENCES**

Ansur REV

**QUERENT'S
INFLUENCE
ON WORLD**

Eolh REV

THE SIGEL READING

THIS RUNE-CAST SHOWS HOW YOU CAN TAILOR THE
LAYOUT ITSELF TO THE SUBJECT MATTER OF THE
QUESTION. THIS READING IS IN THE SHAPE OF THE
RUNE SIGEL (ᛋ), BECAUSE THE QUERENT IS LOOKING
FOR VICTORY IN A CONFLICT.

In this rune-cast, some of
the runes are read more
than once. Different aspects
of their meanings might be
revealed depending partly on
their position, but mainly on
which other runes they are
being linked with.

The bottom three runes
represent the current
situation. Ken (ᚲ) is a torch
giving light and clear sight,
and its reversal means that
the querent cannot see
victory (shown by Sigel) in
the problems over his home
(shown by Odel, ᛟ).

The middle three runes
represent the best course
to follow – Odel, Ger (ᛋ),
and Peorth (ᛈ) reversed,
therefore, home, harvest, and
reversed fate. The reversed
Peorth could simply mean

bad luck, but because Peorth
usually means using the game
pieces of life with great skill
and dexterity, it might be
suggesting that it will not be
an easy fight, and that the
querent may also need
considerable luck. Ger relates
to business contracts about
the home (shown by Odel).
Therefore, the reversed
Peorth could also be
suggesting that the querent
waits and sees what happens
in regard to contracts or
business relationships.

The outcome, shown by
the top three runes, looks
negative. Wyn (ᚹ) means joy,
but the lack of protection of
the reversed Eolh (ᛉ) and
the bad luck of the reversed
Peorth suggest that Wyn will
be negated. There is unlikely
to be any joy.

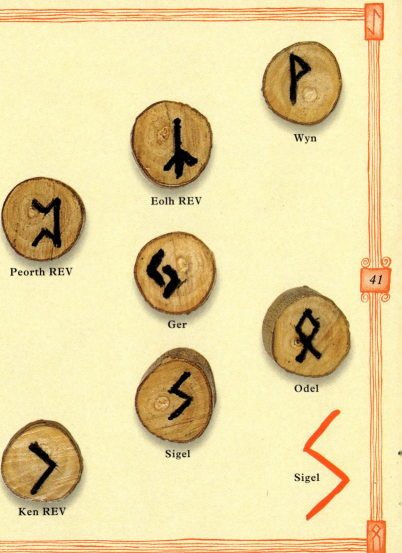

Wyn

Eolh REV

Peorth REV

Ger

Odel

Sigel

Sigel

Ken REV

THE **PEORTH** READING

THIS RUNE-CAST IS IN THE SHAPE OF PEORTH, THE RUNE OF FATE. IT SHOWS YOUR PAST, PRESENT, AND FUTURE, AND LOOKS AT THE PHYSICAL, EMOTIONAL, AND SPIRITUAL. THE QUERENT WANTS TO KNOW WHICH AREAS OF HER LIFE NEED MOST ATTENTION.

In the past, the querent's life path (Rad, ᚱ) has been unprotected (Eolh, ᛉ, reversed). Gyfu (ᚷ), usually a gift, is here related to obligations. The querent feels uncertain (Lagu, ᛚ, reversed), and this will affect her life and her home (Odel, ᛟ).

The physical, emotional, and spiritual aspects of the querent's life are represented by triangles of runes. The lower arm of Peorth (ᚲ) shows the physical. Her life path (Rad), shown with strength (Ur, ᚢ) and victory (Sigel, ᛋ), suggests a challenge being overcome. The emotional is shown by the central rune of the upright stalk and the middle runes of the two arms: Gyfu, Ken (ᚲ), and Sigel – a gift, a torch, and a victory. Here,

Gyfu represents a romantic partnership. It will be illuminated by Ken and Sigel's victory of light over darkness. The spiritual is shown by the triangle of Peorth's upper arm. Here, Odel represents the spiritual home, Ken brings the light of truth, and Ehwaz (ᛗ) shows spiritual advancement.

Eolh reversed and Lagu reversed, the only runes not in the personal triangles, show that the querent's negative life path is being disturbed by external forces. All is therefore not lost. The present moment, shown by Gyfu, can truly become a gift and an opportunity, because from the rest of this reading, the querent is certainly strong enough to take more control of her own life.

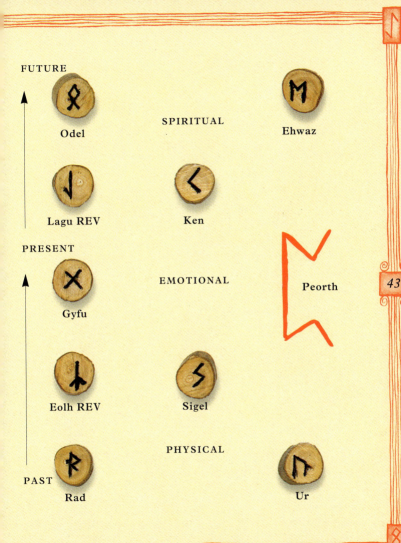

FUTURE

Odel

SPIRITUAL

Ehwaz

Lagu REV

Ken

PRESENT

Gyfu

EMOTIONAL

Peorth

Eolh REV

Sigel

PAST

Rad

PHYSICAL

Ur

RUNE-SCRIPT

A RUNE-CAST CAN GIVE AN INDICATION OF THE FUTURE, AND THIS PROCESS CAN BE REVERSED IN A RUNE-SCRIPT. SPECIFIC RUNES CAN BE SELECTED AND PLACED TOGETHER IN A RUNE-SCRIPT IN ORDER TO ATTRACT A DESIRED FUTURE.

Runes stand for the fundamentals in life, such as the home, protection, wealth, and cooperation. It is possible to put several runes (usually three, five, or seven) together to spell out what you want to happen in your life. Choose the runes carefully, write them in the best order,

ATTRACTING MONEY
Daeg (ᛗ, growth), Feoh (ᚠ, wealth), and Odel (ᛟ, possessions) can be used to attract money.

and be aware of the effect they have on each other. For example, Is (|) "freezes" or preserves the effect of the previous rune, and Feoh (ᚠ) increases the effect of the preceding rune. Write the runes on a piece of paper or scratch them on a sliver of wood. Keep the rune-script with you for a few days, either on your person or under your pillow.

Often the act of preparing a rune-script can put you in the right frame of mind to bring about the desired event yourself. Once the rune-script has achieved its ends, whether through magic or

ROMANTIC SCRIPT
To improve a relationship, use Beorc (ᚦ) to represent sexual love, followed by Ehwaz (ᛗ) for trust and faithfulness, Ger (ᛋ) for bountiful fruitfulness, Feoh (ᚠ) to increase the power of these three runes, and Is (|) to preserve them.

your own efforts, burn it carefully to seal off the magic. When you burn the rune-script, remember to thank the runes for their work on your behalf.

LUCKY BUSINESS
For luck in business, Gyfu (ᚷ) gives the sense of mutual obligation. Follow this with Man (ᛗ) for cooperation, and Ing (◇) for a successful conclusion.

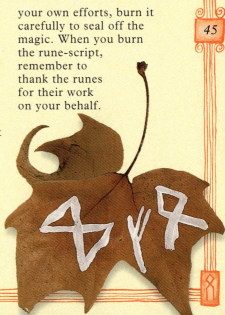

BIND-RUNES

AN ATTRACTIVE WAY OF CARRYING THE POWER OF THE RUNES AROUND WITH YOU IS TO WEAR BIND-RUNES AS JEWELRY. BIND-RUNES CAN BE USED, FOR EXAMPLE, AS AN AMULET FOR PROTECTION AGAINST DANGER, OR TO ATTRACT LOVE OR SUCCESS.

Simple but powerful magic can be achieved by a bind-rune. To make a bind-rune, choose and bind together several runes to bring about a desired effect.

Choose the runes carefully, and consider the effect they might have on each other. Unlike a rune-script, the runes in a bind-rune can be put in any order, because they are going to be combined into a pattern. When choosing the runes, think carefully about what you want the bind-rune to achieve, but also consider the design. Try to make it interesting, attractive, and pleasing; experiment on paper first, and superimpose the various runes on top of each other.

To avoid the design of the bind-rune becoming messy and confusing, it is best to use no more than three

LOVE
BIND-RUNE
To preserve a loving relationship, combine Wyn (ᚹ) with Gyfu (ᚷ), which will give Is (ᛁ).

runes. The size of the bind-rune is not important, but each rune should be to the same scale. The pattern of the bind-rune does not need to be symmetrical. However, to make an attractive design, you can rotate the runes left to right, but not top to bottom.

～ ๑ ～

Making a bind-rune requires creativity and personal involvement, and your intent when making your bind-rune is just as important as the runes you select or how you fit them together. If you are given a bind-rune, or if you buy one, it is always best to know the person who made it. If you make a bind-rune for someone else, make it with love, just as if you were preparing a special meal for that person. It is also a good idea to explain to them what elements you have integrated into your design, and why.

～ ๑ ～

Bind-runes can be carved or painted onto a flat wooden or metal pendant, or if you are skilled at making jewelry, try making a bind-rune by twisting silver wire. Many runes have a central vertical line, but if your particular

HOME PROTECTION

This bindrune combines Eolh (ᛉ) for protection and Odel (ᛟ) for the home. It gives Is (ᛁ), which will preserve protection, and two Thorns (ᚦ), which can act as a defensive hedge around your home.

combination does not, you can add it to the pattern. Remember that you are adding the rune Is (ᛁ), which will preserve the effects of the other combined runes. To aid the design of the bind-rune, you can also add a horizontal baseline, or set the whole pattern inside a circle.

GEMSTONE
A S S O C I A T I O N S

GEMSTONES HAVE TRADITIONAL MEANINGS IN MANY
ANCIENT RELIGIONS. CARRY THE APPROPRIATE
GEMSTONE AROUND WITH YOU, ACCORDING TO THE
RUNIC ASSOCIATIONS THAT YOU ARE SEEKING.

**MOSS
AGATE**
*Feoh is
associated with
moss agate,
which has both
medicinal and
talismanic virtues.*

CARBUNCLE
*Ur is linked with
the carbuncle,
which reputedly
brings success
and energy.*

SAPPHIRE
*Thorn's gem is
the sapphire. Its
color is linked
with the heavens
and holiness.*

EMERALD
*Ansur is
linked with
emeralds, which
have properties of
hidden knowledge
and are considered
beneficial for
the eyes.*

CHRYSOPRASE
*Rad's gemstone
is the greenish
chrysoprase.*

BLOODSTONE
*Traditionally, the
bloodstone,
Ken's gemstone,
has magical
curative powers to stop
bleeding from wounds.*

OPAL
Gyfu's stone, the opal, is linked with friendship, but it should not be used selfishly to try to bring love.

DIAMOND
The hardest gemstone is the diamond, Wyn's stone. Its purity and clarity make it a symbol of truth, love, and commitment.

ONYX
The onyx is associated with Hagal. Black onyx gives spiritual strength, and red-brown onyx protects against pain.

LAPIS LAZULI
Nyd's stone is the deep blue lapis lazuli, which is associated with selfless love and faithful friendship. It gives courage in adversity, especially if you are timid or depressed.

CARNELIAN
Ger's stone, the carnelian, is particularly useful as a talisman to ward off all evil, especially ill health.

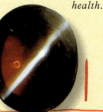

CAT'S-EYE
Is's gemstone, the cat's-eye, protects the wearer against the terrors of night, and is believed to attract and protect wealth.

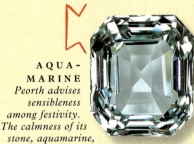

TOPAZ
Eoh's gemstone, the topaz, calms anger and encourages restful sleep.

AQUA-MARINE
Peorth advises sensibleness among festivity. The calmness of its stone, aquamarine, can prove helpful. It is a stone of purity and mysticism.

AMETHYST
Eolh's gem, the amethyst, guards against intoxication, gives calmness in danger, and encourages trust.

RUBY
Sigel's stone, the fiery ruby, is said to protect against attacks, and to warn against poison or impending danger by losing its brilliance.

CORAL
Tyr's gemstone is coral, which has been used in many societies to cure ailments of the throat and digestive system.

MOONSTONE
The calm, harmonious moonstone is linked with Beorc. It can help in romantic relationships and decision-making.

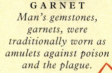

ICELAND SPAR
*Ehwaz is associated
with Iceland spar
(a transparent calcite)
when upright, and with
malachite when reversed.*

GARNET
*Man's gemstones,
garnets, were
traditionally worn as
amulets against poison
and the plague.*

PEARL
*Lagu's gem, the pearl,
symbolizes purity,
strength, and tears,
and is considered
unlucky for lovers.*

AMBER
*Ing's gem is
amber, which
is often worn
around the
throat to
protect against
chills because of
its warmth.*

CHRYSOLITE
*Daeg's gems are
diamonds and
chrysolites, both
of which are
worn for their
brightness
and their
beauty.*

RUBY
*Odel's stone, the
ruby, attracts
friends and
fortune,
and
protects
from evil.*

FLOWER
A S S O C I A T I O N S

WHEN TENDING FLOWERS, HAVE THEIR RELATED RUNES
WITH YOU, AND KEEP THEIR MEANING IN YOUR MIND
TO AID THEIR GROWTH. WHEN GIVING FLOWERS, YOU
CAN CHOOSE THEM BY THEIR RUNIC ASSOCIATIONS.

LILY-OF-THE-VALLEY
Feoh's flower, the lily-of-the-valley, is used to treat heart complaints.

NASTURTIUM
Ur's flower is the nasturtium, which is good for the blood and the digestion.

HONESTY
Justice is one of the attributes of the god Thorn, and honesty is Thorn's flower.

MORNING GLORY
Ansur is linked with morning glory, which encourages wisdom.

SNAPDRAGON
Rad's flower, the snapdragon, encourages journeys and progress.

GORSE FLOWER
The yellow color of the gorse flower symbolizes the illumination of Ken and its creative fire.

WORMWOOD
Gyfu's flower, wormwood, is beneficial for coughs.

LARKSPUR
Wyn's flower is larkspur, or love-in-the-mist. It can be used to help emotional problems.

FERN
The fern is associated with Hagal. It can be used for coughs and chest complaints, but only if it is properly prepared.

CROCUS
The rune Nyd represents all necessities, and its flower, the crocus, can be planted for security in and around your home.

CORNFLOWER
Ger is the rune of harvest and fruit-fulness. Its brilliant blue flower, as its name suggests, is often found in cornfields.

SWEET PEA
The rune Is is linked with the sweet pea, and symbolizes relationships with other people.

LILAC
The sweet-smelling and attractive lilac is linked with Eoh.

CHRYSANTHEMUM
Peorth's characteristics of fate and festivity are associated with the chry-santhemum.

SEDGE
Eolh is shaped like the elk-sedge or elongated sedge plant, and is linked with the more common rush of the same family.

ST. JOHN'S WORT
Sigel is linked with St. John's wort, which is known for healing wounds.

MOONFLOWER
The moonflower is Beorc's flower, and represents renewal, fertility, and birth.

RED-HOT POKER
Tyr, the original god of war and justice, is associated with the red-hot poker. Tyr is also the god of male sexuality.

FORSYTHIA
Ehwaz's flower, the forsythia, is a symbol of change.

FOXGLOVE
Man's flower, the foxglove, is extremely poisonous. However, if properly used in medicine, it can help with circulatory problems.

WATER LILY
Lagu, the rune of water, is linked with the water lily. It is particularly useful for poultices.

GENTIAN
Ing is linked with gentians, which can aid the digestion.

SNOWDROP
Sometimes called the "flowers of hope," snowdrops are associated with the rune Odel.

POT MARIGOLD
Daeg is linked with the pot marigold, an excellent plant for healing bruises.

TREE
ASSOCIATIONS

PARTICULAR TREES HAVE LINKS WITH MANY OF THE
RUNES AND THE NORSE GODS. CARRY THE APPROPRIATE
TREE'S BLOSSOM, BARK, TWIG, OR LEAF ACCORDING TO
THE RUNIC ASSOCIATIONS THAT YOU ARE SEEKING.

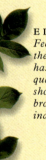

ELDER
*Feoh's tree is
the elder. It
has protective
qualities, but
should not be
brought
indoors.*

BIRCH
*Ur's tree, the birch,
brings good fortune
to a house.*

ASH
*Ansur, the god-
rune, is linked
to the ash
tree, the
World Tree.*

HAWTHORN
*The rune Thorn
is linked to
thorn-bearers such
as the hawthorn.*

OAK
*Rad's tree, the
oak, is a sacred
tree throughout
northern Europe.*

PINE
*Ken's tree, the
pine, makes
excellent purifying
incense, and
represents
enlightenment.*

56

ELM
Gyfu's trees are the elm, particularly the wych elm, and the ash.

ASH
Wyn's tree, the ash, is the name of the Norse equivalent of Adam, the first man, who was made from an ash tree.

YEW
The rune Hagal is associated with both the yew and the ash tree.

MOUNTAIN-ASH
Nyd's trees are mountain-ash, which is often used to protect the home, and the beech.

ALDER
The tree associated with Is is the alder. Its wood is long-lasting, and is traditionally used in foundations of buildings, or for making charcoal.

OAK
Ger's tree, the oak, is believed to protect the home against lightning.

YEW
Eoh's tree, the yew, is a highly poisonous tree, associated with the passage to the next world.

ASPEN
Peorth's associated trees are the aspen and beech.

YEW
The protective rune Eolh is linked with the yew tree. Its wood is traditionally used for making longbows.

JUNIPER
Sigel's tree, the juniper, protects against harm.

58

OAK
Tyr's tree is the powerful and sacred oak, the tree of the sky-god.

BIRCH
Beorc's tree, the birch, is sacred to the Mother-goddess.

ASH
The rune Ehwaz is linked with both the ash and the oak.

HOLLY
Man's tree, the holly, is said to protect doorways from evil intruders.

WILLOW
Lagu's tree is the water-loving and sorrowful willow.

APPLE
The fertile apple tree is associated with the rune Ing.

HAWTHORN
Odel's tree, the hawthorn, makes a good protective hedge around the home.

SPRUCE
The tree of the rune Daeg is the evergreen spruce.

INDEX

ACKNOWLEDGMENTS

Artwork
Anna Benjamin

Special Photography
Steve Gorton

Additional Photography
Sue Atkinson, Deni Bown, Jane Burton, Peter Chadwick,
Gordon Clayton, Geoff Dann, Stephen Hayward,
Jacqui Hurst, Colin Keates, Roger Phillips, Tim Ridley,
Harry Taylor, Kim Taylor, Matthew Ward.

Editorial assistance Martha Swift,
Picture research assistance Ingrid Nilsson,
DTP design assistance Daniel McCarthy.

The publisher would like to thank the following for
their kind permission to reproduce rune cards:

Phoenix Runes, and Anglo-Saxon Books for *Rune Cards and Anglo-Saxon
Mythology, Migration & Magic* by Tony Linsell;
illustrated by Brian Partridge.

Picture Credits

Key: *t* top; *c* center; *b* below; *l* left; *r* right

British Museum 15*t*; Bruce Coleman/Dries van Zyl 20*cl*; Danish National
Museum 4*c*, 11*tl*, *br*; CM Dixon 13*r*; ET Archive 9*r*; Werner Forman
Archive/Statens Historiska Museum, Stockholm 5*c*, 14*b*, 24*cl*; Images Color
Library 8*c*, 12*bl*, 13*tl*; Harry Smith Collection 52*crb*, 54*bl*, *c*; Statens Historika
Museum, Stockholm 10*bl*; Tony Stone Images/Ron Dahlguist 26*tr*.